Stardust Bruises & Dewdrop Delirium

Tiffany Ruby

BookLeaf Publishing

India | USA | UK

Presentation by *BookLeaf Publishing*

Web: www.bookleafpub.com

E-mail: info@bookleafpub.com

ISBN: 9789360940867

First edition 2024

To my babies, keep doing you and you will do amazing things. Gigi and Grumpybear, everything I am is because of you.

ACKNOWLEDGEMENT

To J & D,
Thank you for putting up with my silliness and
continuing to support my madness.

Solace

She stole night
From the empty sky,
Held it close,
Took it out
When she needed dark comfort
Wrapped tight around her

Bewilderment

2

Disappearing
Into the fog
Trailing wisps clouding mind
Only silk threads,
Gossamer thin
Of the path left behind

Thickening haze
Misty edges
Confusion undefined
Lost in haar's thick
Cold light, obscured
Gloomy miasma blinds

Aching Princess

Broken wings
Pray to belong
Still singing
Sad bird songs

Tempest Screams

Drowning under a tide of words
Tsunami waves of ink
Crash violently against emotion's shores
Rocky storms speak unheard
Liquid thoughts swirl, hurricane script
Implores

Grief's Verity

5

Hope is a grim truth
Hidden behind flowered lies
Watching for moments
Of weakness, enveloping
The world, suddenly seen blind

Watercolour Heart

6

Her soft, watercolour heart
Leaked pastel sentiments
Silver feather works of art
Her soft, watercolour heart
Moon dreams did she impart
Peony poems a souls fragment
Her soft, watercolour heart
Leaked pastel sentiments

Equilibrium

7

Thunder quiets
Storms in her mind
Wild water runs
Soothing her tempestuous nerves
Lightning makes her feel alive as
Wild water runs

Silent Realm

Snow glitters
Falling off the silver moon, full
Like plummeting wish stars
Dusting frozen trees
Ethereal
Spells enthral

Rectitude

9

She came to crossroads of the end
Wearing her fanciest
Shade of night, to match the stains on her soul
Proof survivors portend,
She stole the strength of dawn's rising
Heart smiles whole

Thunderstorm Soul

Ghost lines etched on
Thunderstorm soul
Torrents of darkness churns
Erupting starlight
Bright from under
Unknown waters nocturne

Contorted night
Envelopes her
Tumbling over sunburn
Impact reaches
In retrospect
As her heart of caged lightning yearns

Dusk Demeanour

She was darkness
Satin, flowing grace
Untamed
Midnight
Moonlight mystery
Shadowed beauty

Reverie

Ink whispering gentle thoughts sage
Tales of emotional rampage
Coloured words sing, bloody soul cage
Page upon page,
Page upon page

Winsome

At the edges of inspiration, brain fog glimmers
Disquieted ambition on dialogue glimmers

Older and colder, her hope danced
Thousand memories on youth's catalogue
glimmers

Smokey silhouette twirling wispy shadows
Colliding finite time, infinities smog glimmers

Clouded battles reflect on rusted iron bubbles
Pride muddled on monologue glimmers

Musky fragrance, whiskey deep haze
She shed their veil as Ruby snakeskin unclogs
glimmers

Strychnine Siren

Flowers whispered
Poisoned honey
Sang wordless tunes
Of murder with her ravens black
Dancing to purple skies demise
Sang wordless tunes

Temptation's Penchant

15

Faded opulence
Fuchsia petal waterfalls
Love letter saga
Candlelit seasons burn slow
Illustrious lullabies

Dissociation

Ill-intentions
Thick and cloying
Mindless soul loose
Confusion permeates being
Frenetic disconnection shrieks
Mindless soul loose

Finding Herself

Emptiness inside
Unspeakable things were done
Needing to fill it
Until she realised the truth
That was where she hid safely

Stygian Burial

Patchwork darkness
Shadow threads tether
Held together
Uneven gloom

Lights spark starkness
Ashen smoke feathers
Coal skies aether
Volcanic doom

Acceptance Begged

19

Tears in her eyes and a stone heart
She presents her treasure
Pink innocence, waits response, roiling grey
Stress piled up, lover's part
Standing exposed, purple pain paints
Her doomsday

Bitter Arctic Wilds

Upon frozen blade
Summer's culling comes quickly
Withering blossom's
Wounds cauterised chaos numb
Protective warmth forsaken

Celosia

Forest
Fire born
Crimson drenched embers
Charred

Moon Songs

Her haunting voice
Trails over skin
Tingling within
Melody's kiss

Moon songs rejoice
Sensual din
Elusive grin
Lyrics soft bliss

Woman Untamed

She did not fear
Wild beast stalking shadows
She felt kinship,
Drawn to their untamed
nature, fierce her heart
beat, seeking escape from life's daily cage
to run free in savage forest feral

She did not fear
The primitive howling
of wolves on the wind,
Her own lamenting
soul sang, unbroken
Her power wailing under the full moon
Twinkling ubiquitous as connection calls

Torrential Maudlin

Glinting moon hides
Behind dirty
Storm clouds, foul weather, thick
Battering wind
Nearing frenzy
Swirling confusion quick

Thunder fist hits
Lightning fingers
Close on sodden ground slick
Aberrant sound
Foreboding sense
Disquieting homesick

Downward Spiral

Bent to breaking
Dead leaves drifting
Downward spiral
Listening to the stars singing
Million chimes trilling from the sky
Downward spiral

Release

Speak
The nightmare
Rob its power
Collapse the terror tomb
Beautiful

Foreboding

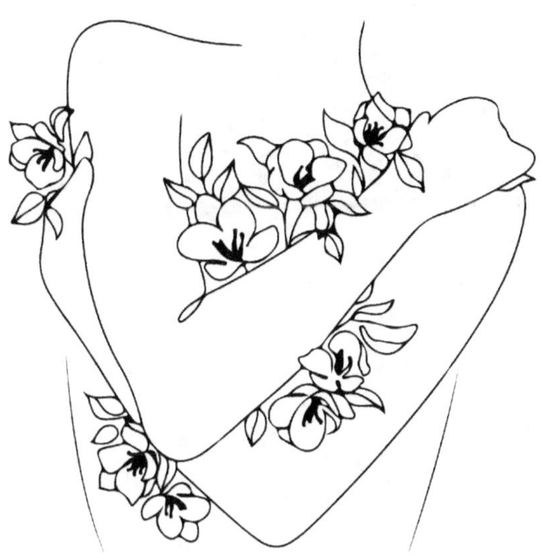

Hopeful
She held the rain
Delicate drops cradled
Awaiting the bubble to pop
Fearful

Remembrance

Her fragrance lingers
Unique blend
Memory bringer
Her scent mends

Just perceptible
Her scent mends
Floral semblable
Unique blend

Mist of madness brings
Unique blend
All her little things
Her scent lingers

Nocturnal Evocation

Moon's rampage
Morbid cage
Gorging light
Nocturnal
Frenzied stars
Storm cloud scars
Souls afar
Eternal

Her Nightfall

She wore neon black
Comforted
By flowers at night

Cruel Tomorrow

31

Brittle bones
Splinter under stress
Fragile heart
Unsteady
Ancient manuscript survives
Vintage memories

Collapsing Moon

Pitch black sky falls
Tsunami red
Collapsing moon
Fabric of existence pulling
Apart like tattered carpets thin
Collapsing moon

Winter's Wake

Dark
Snow
Falling
On white night
Lost forest stands still
Breathing grief's ash on empty graves

Mulberry Wind

Mulberry black wings
Stain the moon
Soot birds ride the wind

Brandy Visions

Blood washes upon the sand
Sweet cherry swirls on burning whiskey smoke
Destruction chokes dreamland

Caliginous Stars

Metal moon melting heavy
Liquid mercury stains rain
Night problems collect hardboiled
Caliginous stars scream gritty noir pain

Time Restoring

37

Summer death an angry roaring
Blinded by burning water pouring
Her cold winter eyes imploring
Time restoring,
Time restoring

Let Deluge Drown

Let rain fall
Let the waves crash down
Let water
Flow over
Let the shores flood, levies burst
Let holy sea surge

Cloudburst

Running along clouds,
Falling through stars
Drifting beneath ocean waves
Struggle fading with dusk

Despondent Day

Black rain falls
Splintered sky cries soot
Ash deluge
Pitch rainbow
Hope is syphoned, colourless
Despondent day stains

Withering Brave

Fear coiled a
Silver stranded noose
Tightening
With each breath
Adrenaline increasing
Panicked spasms fight

Grey Moon Saga

Cold days
Shadows collect
Serial mistakes echoing dark days
Familiar bane paints grey moon skeleton
Lost skies
Savage saga
Overcast night

Elucidate

43

Silver river formed constellations line
Celestial conjunction
Clashing galaxy waves

Sunflower Sensitive

Gold pixie dust
Illustrious
Magical dreams
Morning dew drops collect moon beams
Indigo wings flutter glass flight
Magical dreams

Enigma Raw

Glass heart
Sanguine ornament
Crimson casket of carmine ribs protects
Handcrafted trust cracks, fragile and raw
Delicate beating
Murderous weight
Shattered breath

Rose Scented Ice

Frozen florets form
Winter garden
Rose scented ice
Poisoned faerie masquerade ball
Bleeds iris blue verglas bouquet
Rose scented ice

Delicate Strength

47

Flowers
Grown under
Hailstorm assault
Discover bent stalks
Still lend their strength
So, blossoms
Unfurl

Ghostly Creation Cold

48

White satin shadows wrapping, ghostly creation
Protective shroud slithering, around small
shoulders
Warmth dares not satisfy cold, devastating still
Obscure fluid swallowed thick, silky silence
drowns

Eunoia

Summer
Trees weep
Flower petal path

Drops
Sunlit jade
Sparkle during eclipse

Wildflowers
Reflect behind
Her restless eyes

Counting
Endless stars
Her night ends